VIVID STORIES   Bess Rodriguez Richard

VIVID STORIES

Published by: The Artists Archives of the Western Reserve
to accompany the exhibition of the same name

Designed by: Mindy Tousley
Contributors include:
Bess Rodriguez Richard

Photography for Richard is courtesy of the AAWR
Photographic portrait of Richard by Herbert Ascherman Jr, courtesy of AAWR

AAWR Support Staff:
Executive Director: Mindy Tousley
Gallery and Archives Coordinator: Megan Alves
Collections Department: Kelly Pontoni, Edward Valentin Lugo

AAWR Board of Directors:
Philip Bautista, President
Stuart Pearl, Vice President
David Joranko, Treasurer
Jocelyn Ruf, Secretary

Michael Bowen
Stephen Bucchieri
Cris Drugan
Lee Heinen
Suzan Kraus
Dr Vincent Monnier
Rota Sackerlotzky
John Sargent III

Copyright 2018 The Artists Archives of the Western Reserve
All Rights Reserved

VIVID STORIES   Bess Rodriguez Richard

November 16,, 2018 - january 12, 2019

Presented by
The Artists Archives of the Western Reserve
1834 E 123rd St., Cleveland Ohio 44106

Cover image: *San Cristobal Plaza* oil and acrylic on Canvas 30" x 40" 2010

AAWR would like to thank the following supporters:

The Bernice and David Davis Art Foundation
The George Gund Foundation
The William Bingham Foundation
The Zufall Foundation

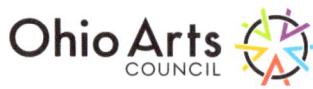

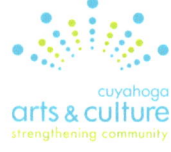

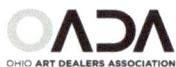

The Artists Archives of the Western Reserve (AAWR) is a unique archival facility and regional museum created to preserve representative bodies of work by Ohio visual artists.

Through ongoing research, exhibition, and educational programs the AAWR actively documents and promotes this cultural heritage for the benefit of the public.

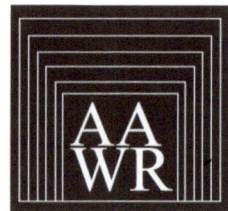

Introduction and Acknowledgments

Bess Rodriguez Richard was accepted into the Archives in December of 2014. She is the 70th artist to be archived and the 35th woman. I am proud to welcome her into the Archives through, *Vivid Stories*, her inaugural solo exhibition.

As the progeny of US diplomats, Bess spent a large portion of her childhood travelling. An artist from the time she was a toddler she expressed an early interest in drawing and a natural affinity for using color in her work. Encouraged in her endeavors by her parents and her primary teachers, Bess began painting in earnest while attending college. In 1979 she spent a summer in Brittany, France developing a keen interest in Plein-air painting under the tutelage of an instructor. Thus began the pattern for her life as an artist; Combining her love of travel and curiosity regarding other cultures, with painting in the moment from life while perfecting her craft under the watchful eyes of a variety of instructors. It was when she was learning color theory from a new teacher that a watershed moment occurred with her painting, "Boom Box Baby". This transitional painting indicates the point where her work changes from realistic renderings of what her eyes are seeing to expressionistic interpretations of her creative state of being as an artist. This marks her real beginnings as a story teller capable of weaving a narrative of place and time through the creative lens of her paintings. Her vibrant colors and textured canvases have prompted some viewers to tell her,"…they would like to step into them and live there". Whether she is painting the landscape, a still life or a portrait, her mature style presents us with a joyous interpretation of life that is hard to resist.

I would like to acknowledge and thank all of those who support the Artists Archives of the Western Reserve, and make exhibitions like this one possible. Thank you to Megan Alves, Gallery and Archives Coordinator, the AAWR Exhibition Committee chaired by John Sargent, as well as all the other members and volunteers including our dedicated Board of Directors. A very special thank you to the David E Davis Art Foundation which has continued to support the dream of our founder, David Davis, for the past twenty one years. Last, but not least, thank you to Bess Rodriguez Richard and all of the other Archived Artists for your contributions to the fabric of our culture, without you the Archives would not have a reason to exist.

Mindy Tousley
AAWR Executive Director

BESS RODRIGUEZ RICHARD

"At less than two years of age I began to draw...in color. I began painting in high school and then in earnest in college. I spent a summer in Brittany, France, after graduating from college and there my keen interest in plein air painting developed. Wherever I have lived, I have always found an art teacher from whom I have gleaned and extracted "Golden nuggets" of wisdom and I have culled these together to form a unique and eclectic form of expressionism which continues to evolve. I have studied art in Japan, California (U.C. Berkeley's extension program); Princeton, New Jersey's Arts Council; Corcoran School of Art in Washington D.C., The Yellow Barn in Glen Echo Maryland; and the Cleveland Institute of Art.

Perhaps due to the bold colors I observed while living in Mexico City as a child, I love to create vibrant pictures. I have been told by some who have viewed my paintings that they would like to step into them and live there. This impulse to create something pleasing or intriguing that captures one's eye coupled with an increasing fascination with color has grown in me. To tell a story, to create a mood, or to evoke...to communicate with kindred spirits...this fuels my creative process. "

Bess Rodriquez Richard 2014

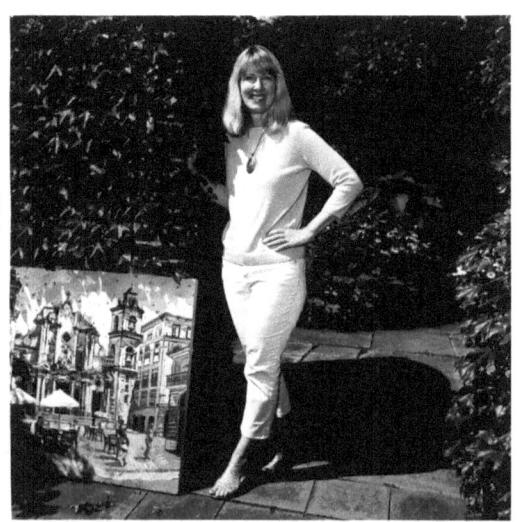

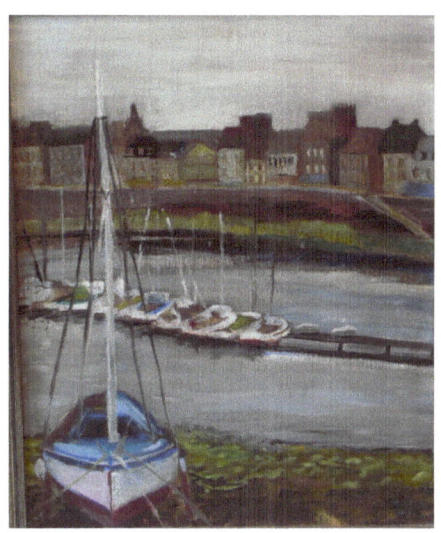

As part of my B.F.A., I spent 6 weeks in Brittany, France enrolled in an advanced landscape painting course (offered at George Washington U.). I learned to paint plein air works in oil. Every morning, at 6:00 a.m., we'd wake to a Captain's bell, eat croissants with confitures, yogurt and hot coffee. Following breakfast, we would drive in jeeps to a site, sometimes first observe a demonstration by our professor and then we could paint. Then, a lunch break, followed by transportation to a new site and afternoon painting.

This is an example of my early work with its muted palette. I set my French easel up on a dock and focused on a sailboat in the foreground and townhouses lined the background. The skies in Brittany were cloudy initially but as the week wore on became cobalt blue.

Camaret, Brittany, France
oil; on canvas 22" x 18" 1979
collection of AAWR

This was a pivotal painting; my work changed dramatically due to two events in my life: the diagnosis of my pre-schooler as autistic and a new teacher, the Director of the Princeton Arts Council, who taught Color Theory in detail. My muted palette and hesitant brushwork became significantly bolder.

My husband upon seeing this painting, gasped and said, "that's equivalent to sitting in your car at a red light and having someone pull up next to you with a blaring radio."

Bess Rodriquez Richard

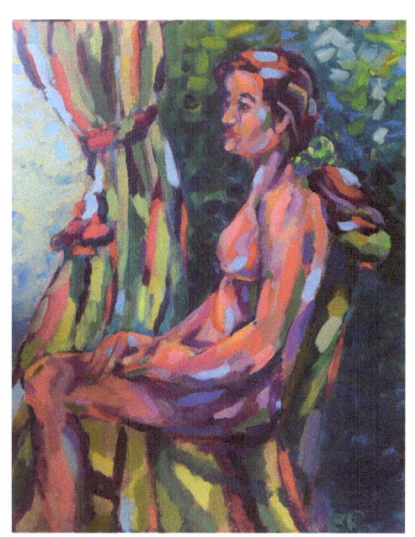

Boom Box Baby
acrylic on canvas 28" x 22" 1995
collection of AAWR

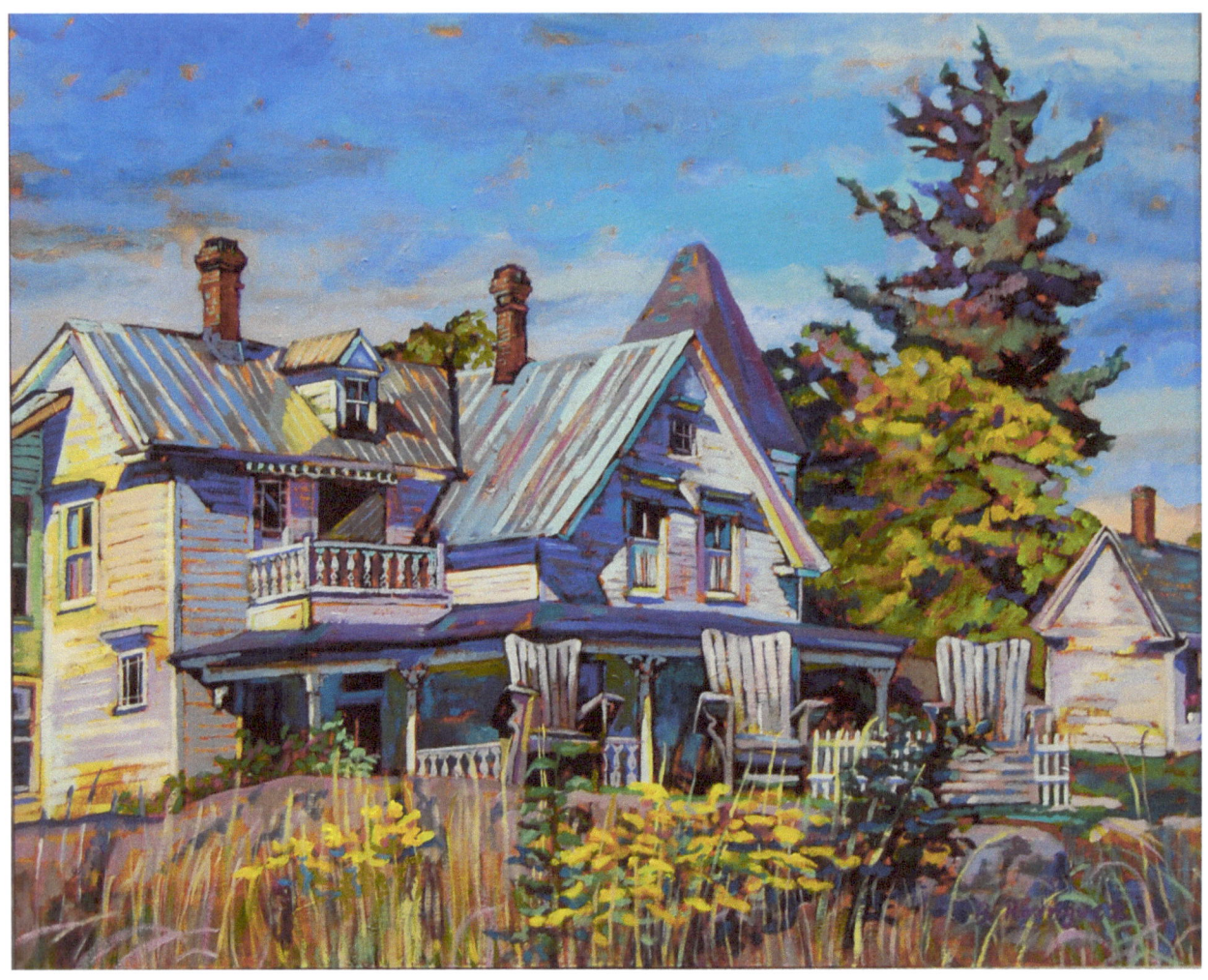

This painting is of a home, possibly a bed and breakfast, perched on a hill overlooking Stonington's harbor. I have always loved Edward Hopper and was inspired by him in this work. I tried to capture his distinctive light and feeling of isolation.

Bess Rodriguez Richard

Stonington, Maine acrylic on canvas 26" x 32" 2005
collection of AAWR

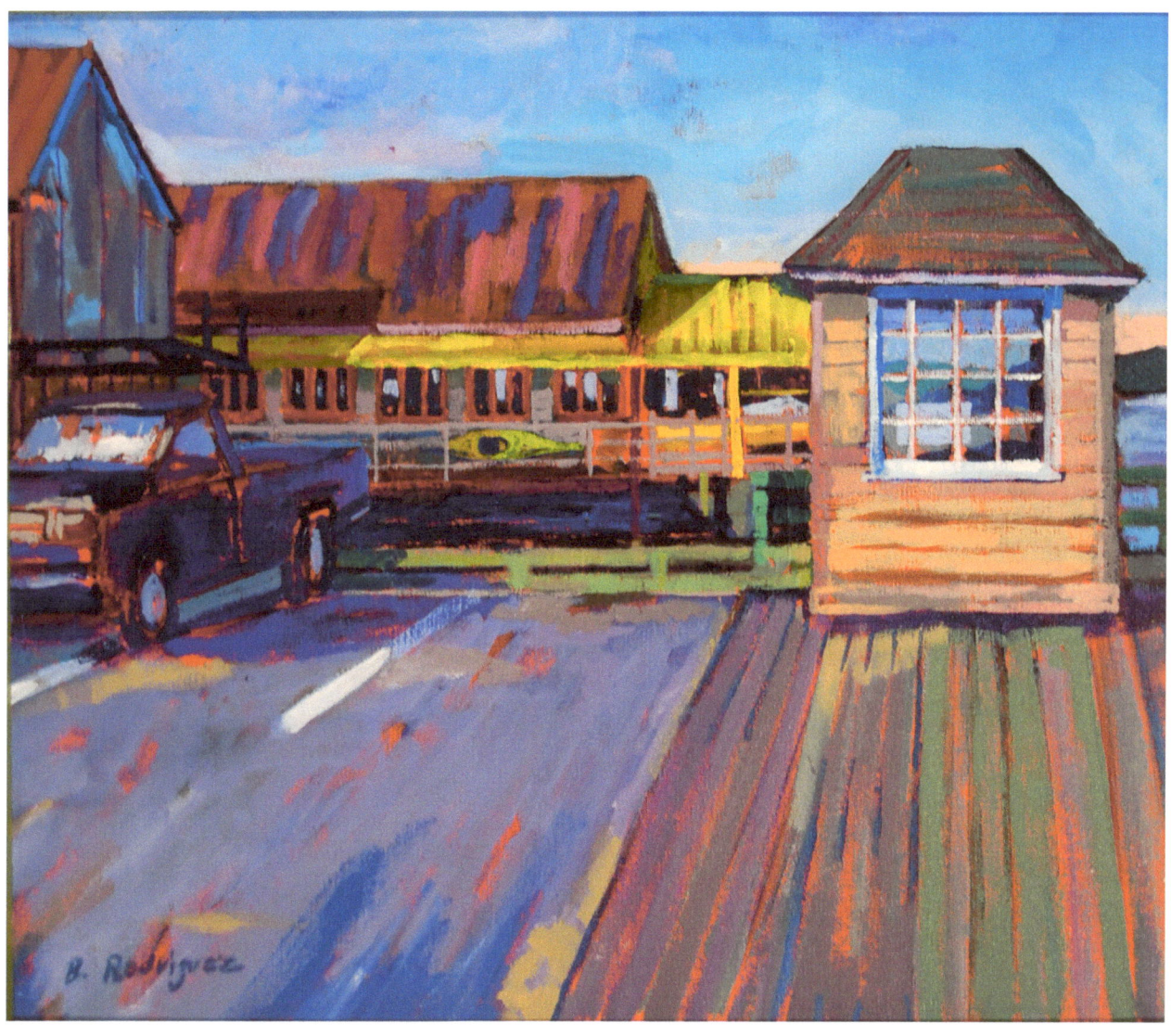

This painting I started outdoors at night and then revised it into a day scene. I was trying to "channel" Edward Hopper, as he's always been one of my favorite artists. I really enjoyed creating a simple composition of geometric shapes. And I liked leaving traces of the black ground throughout the painting.

Bess Rodriguez Richard

Dennet's Fish House, Maine acrylic on canvas board   14" x 18" 2006
collection of the artist

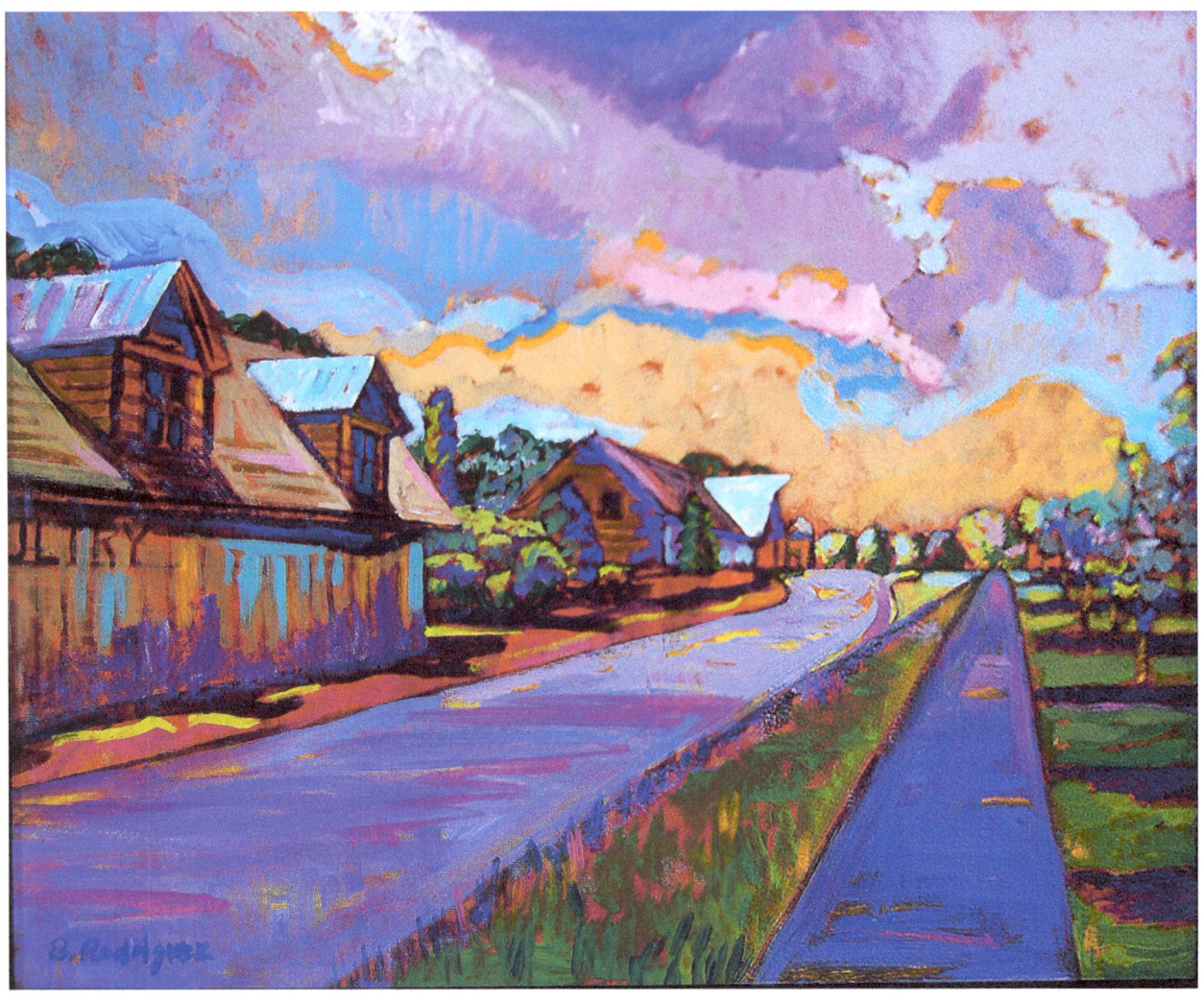

I visited this farm outside Niagara-on-the-Lake. I enjoyed creating an expressive work, playing with the colors in the sky and the clouds and also trying to move one's eye rapidly into the mid ground and then into the background via one-point perspective.

Bess Rodriguez Richard

Farm, Niagara - on - the - Lake, Canada, acrylic on canvas 21" x 25" 2005
collection of the artist

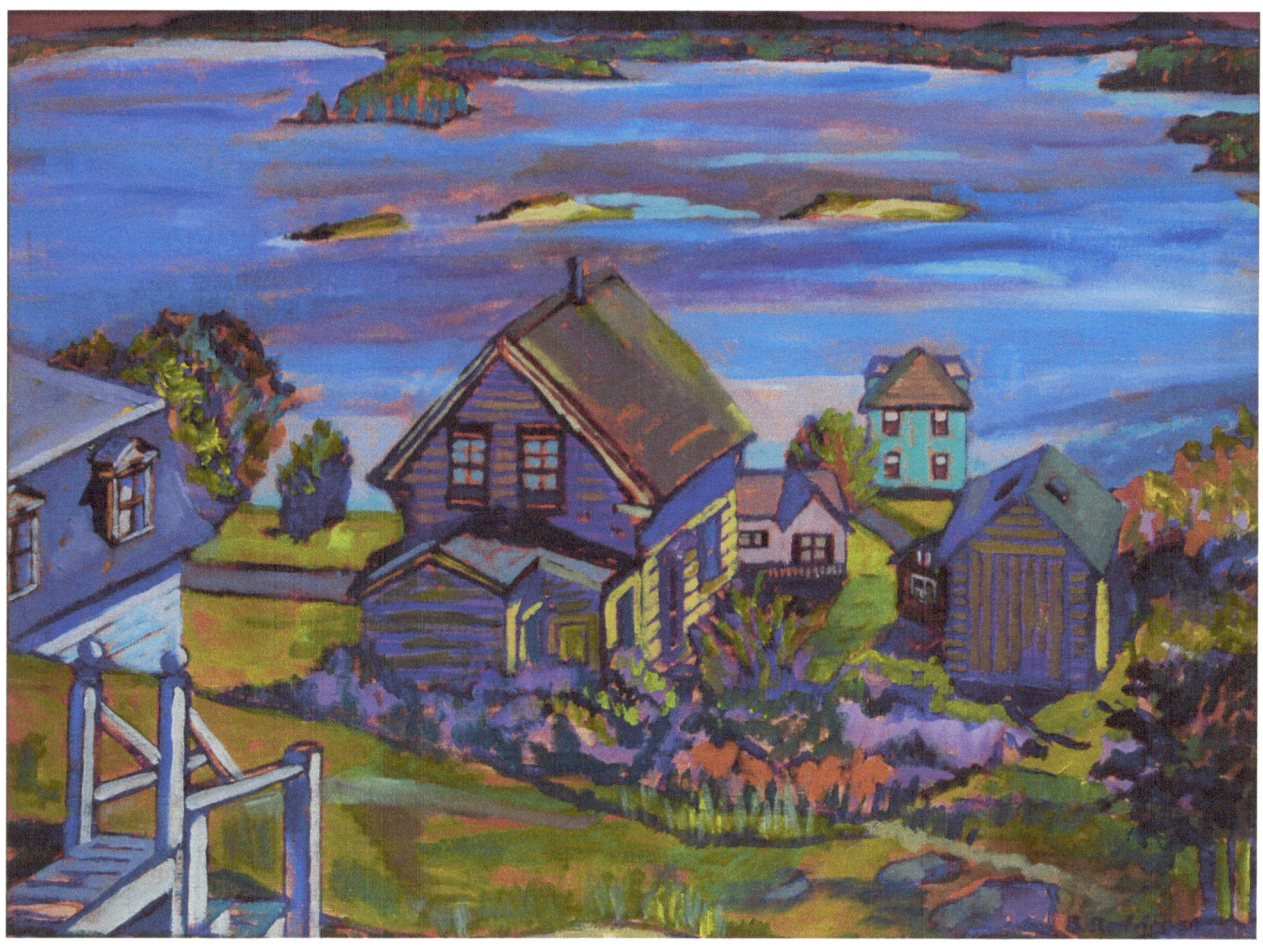

This is a plein air painting done during a one-week workshop in Castine, Maine. I had begun to use warm grounds in my paintings (primarily red or orange). I completed the painting in 5 hours, standing on a rocky hill. The previous year, I painted a similar view and sold it the next day at a show. The owner, a friend of a friend, had been Ambassador to Iceland and had settled in Castine. The following summer, she purchased two more of my Maine plein air paintings; I had returned to Castine and environs for a second summer workshop.

Bess Rodriguez Richard

Overlooking Stonington Harbor, Maine acrylic on canvas 20" x 26" 2005
collection of the AAWR

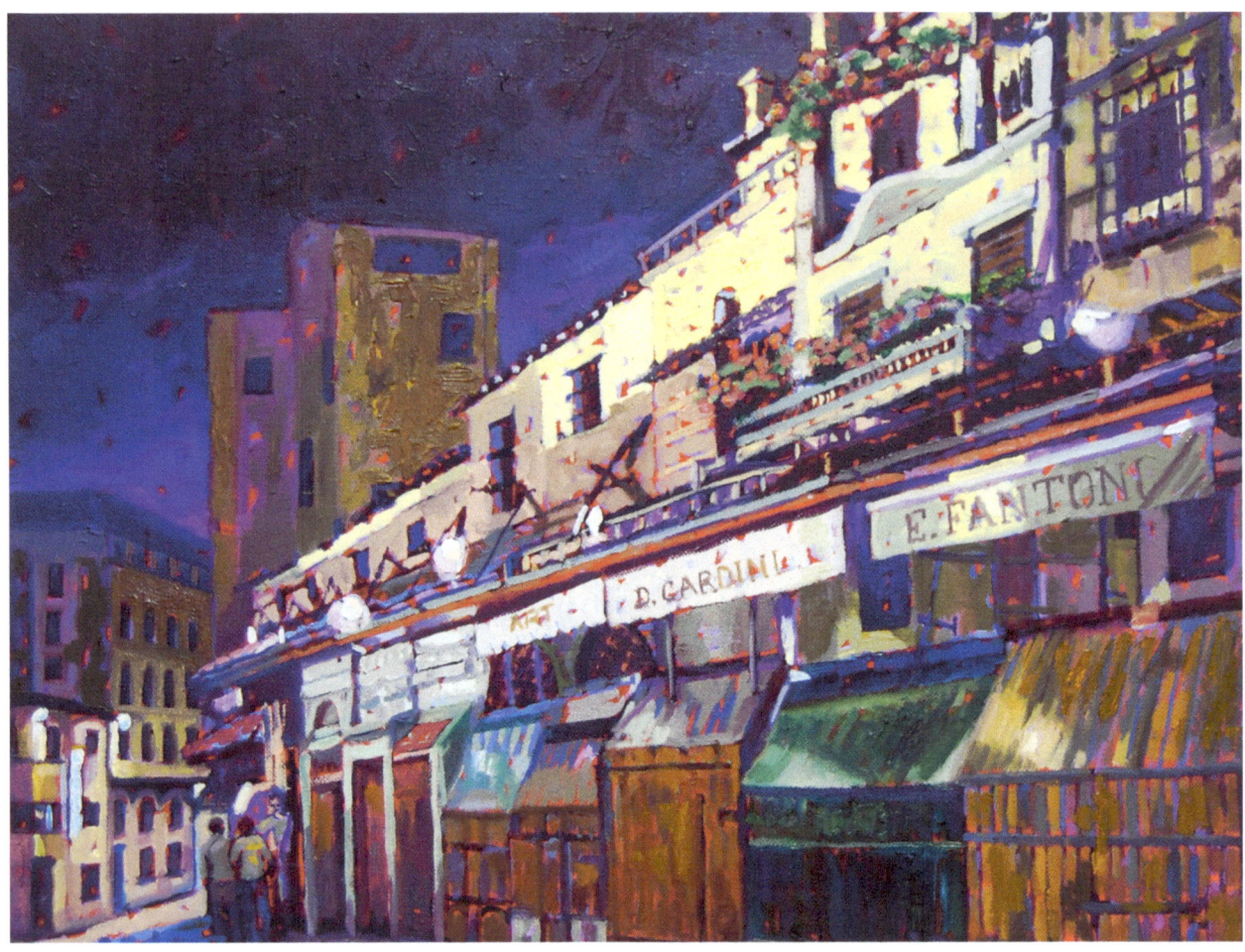

This was my first successful attempt at a night scene. Florence is one of my favorite cities. I feel so at home there. I loved creating this nighttime scene of the bridge with its shops shuttered. And I added in some figures for scale and interest to draw one into the picture.

Bess Rodriguez Richard

Night, Ponte Vecchio, Florence, Italy   oil and acrylic on canvas   16" x 20" 2009
collection of the artist

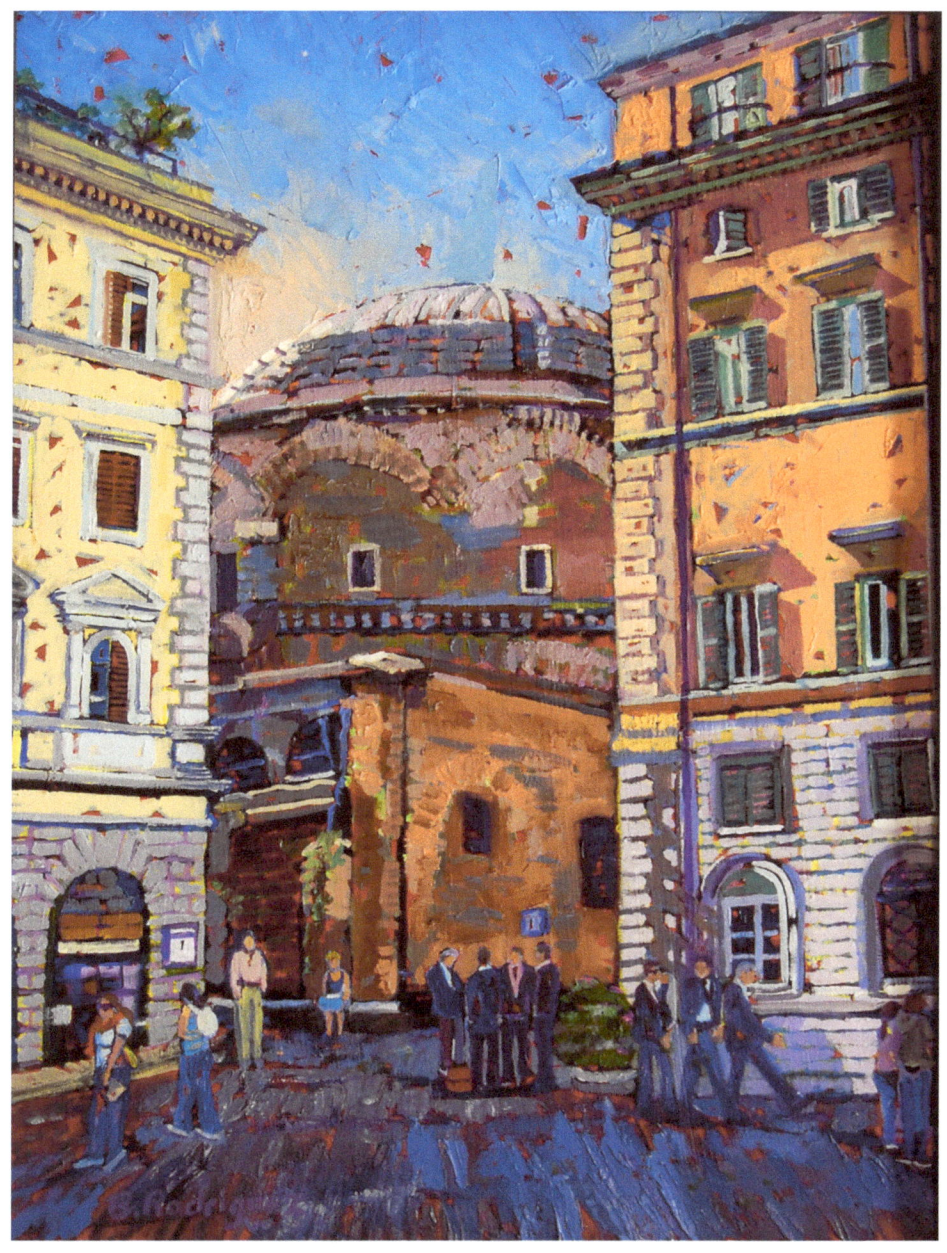

I liked this view of the Pantheon in Rome. It looks like a face looking out, framed by buildings. And I wanted to do a vertical landscape of it to make it more dynamic. I feel it is a small gem and a wonderful memory of my visit there.

Bess Rodriguez Richard

Pantheon Peeking,, Rome, Italy oil on canvas 24" x 18" 2009
collection of the artist

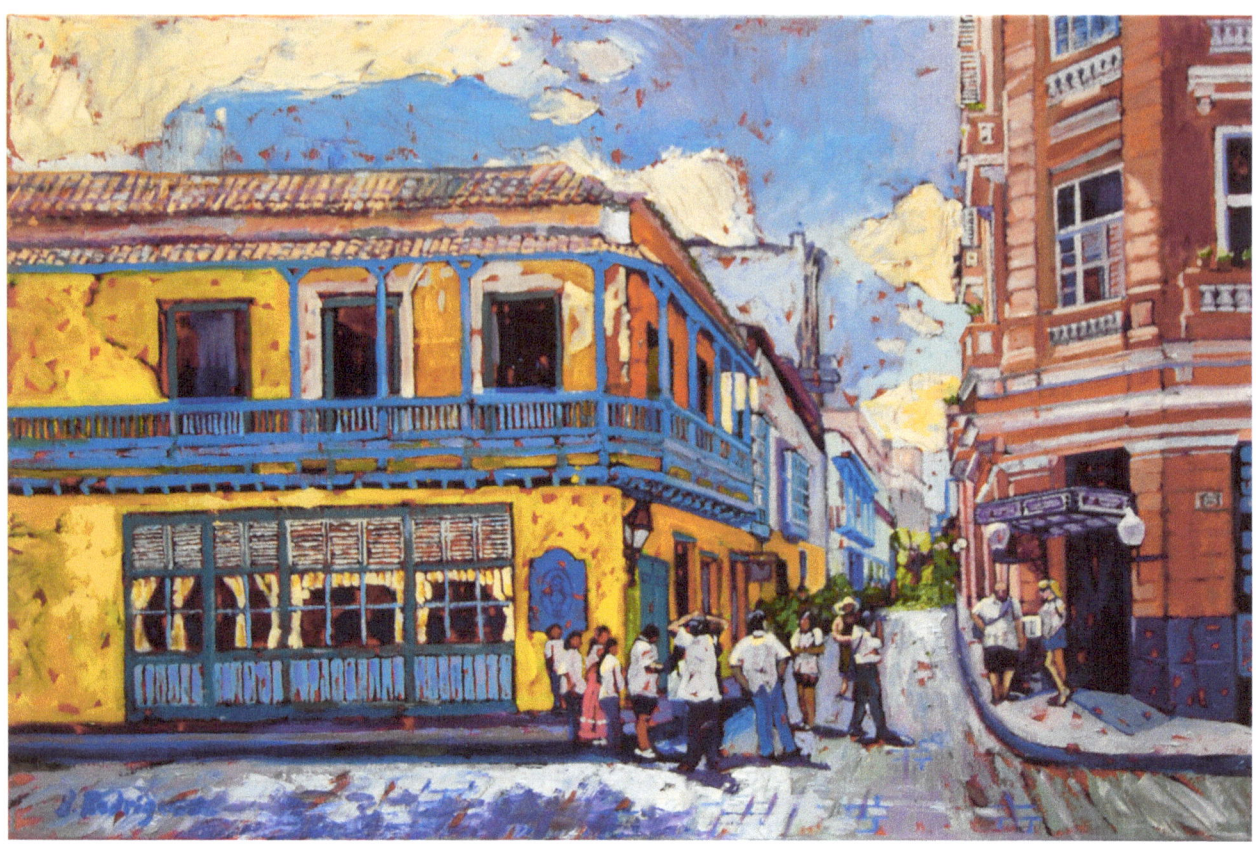

Several years ago, I visited Cuba. I've painted five paintings of that trip. As a bit of trivia, the building on the right, is the Ambos Mundos hotel where Ernest Hemingway was a guest and during his stay wrote the first few chapters of "For Whom the Bell Tolls" in room 551. I strove to capture the bright light and heat of a July summer day in Havana. And I also enjoyed building up the paint with palette knife.

Bess Rodriguez Richard

Old Havana (and a Hemingway haunt) oil and acrylic on canvas 24" x 36" 2010
collection of the artist

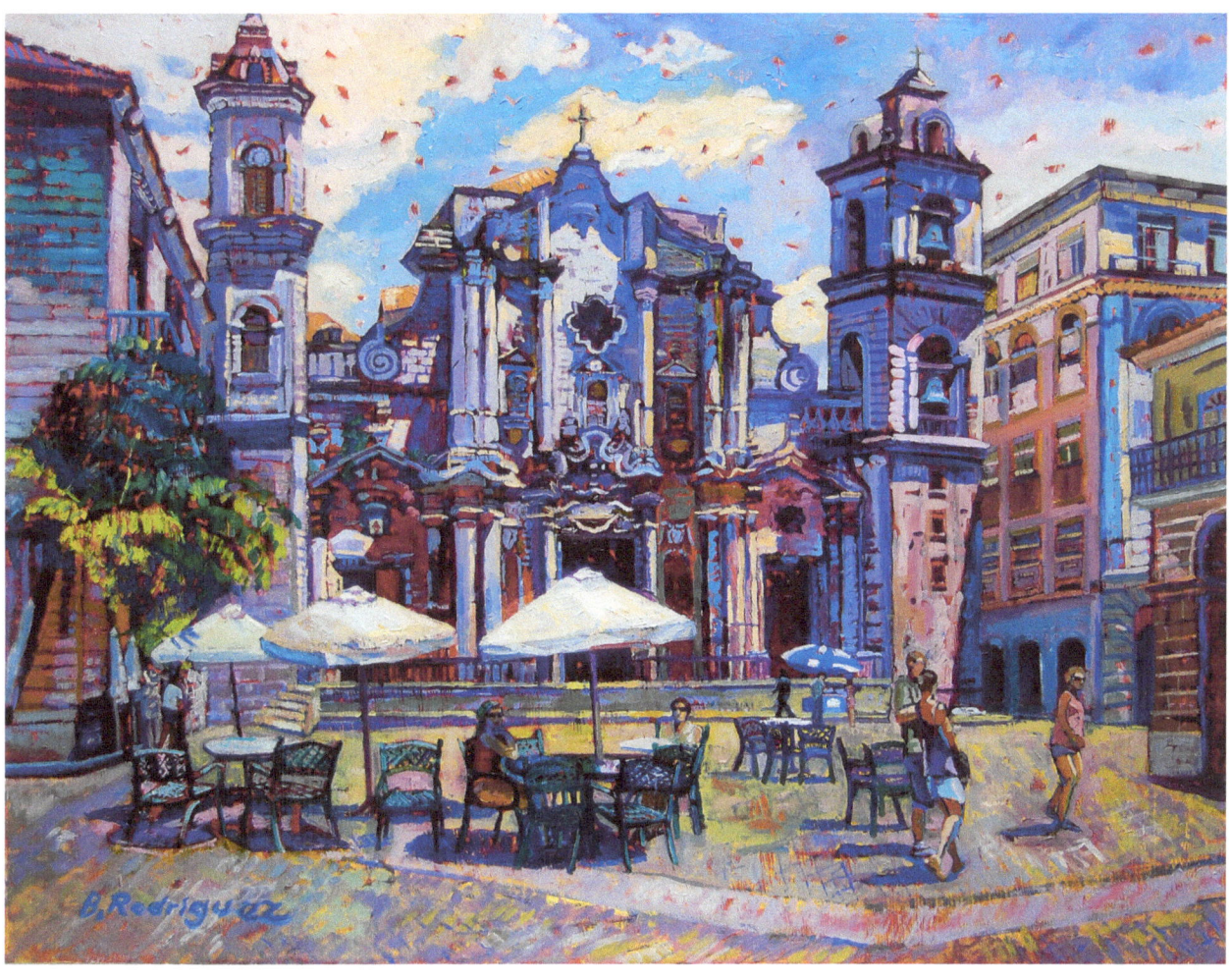

This painting of St. Christopher's cathedral in downtown Havana was particularly challenging to draw due to its Baroque curves, all of the architectural details, and that one tower is wider than the other. I have always loved architecture and took as many architectural history classes in college as were offered. This church, built in the mid- 18th century and said to have held the remains of Christopher Columbus has been described as "Music Set in Stone". It was a labor of love to get the scale of it and to accurately depict the perspective.

Bess Rodriguez Richard

San Cristobal Plaza, Havana, Cuba oil and acrylic on canvas 30" x 40" 2010
collection of the artist

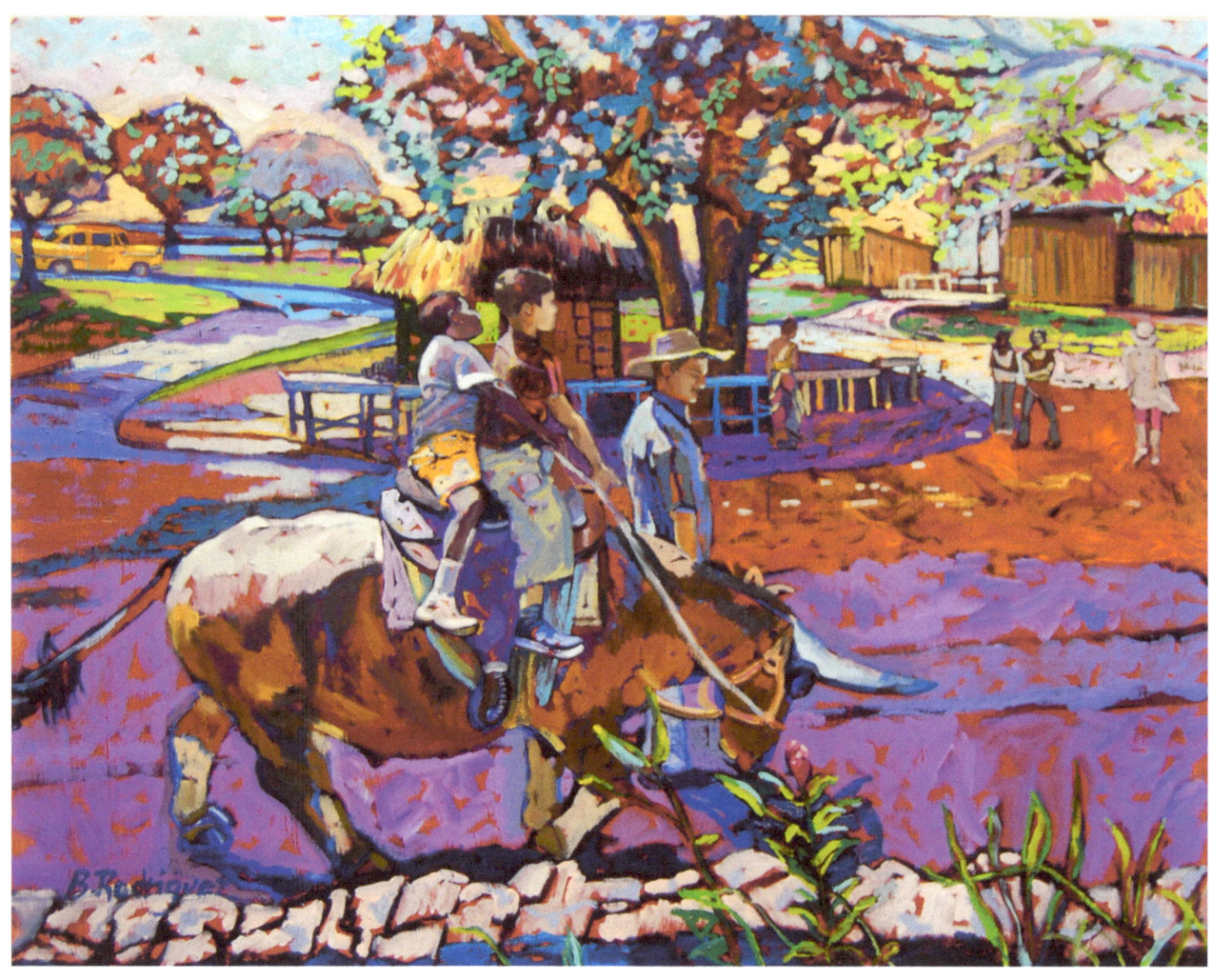

I had the opportunity to visit Cuba in 2009. I created a group of paintings, my Cuba series, and this is one of them. It is set in Vignales, 3 hours west of Havana (the tobacco-growing region). I'd never painted such a large beast, the ox, and was "channeling" Henry Moore when trying to capture it. And in creating this work, I was inspired by the Latin American writers, Gabriel Garcia Marquez and Isabel Allende, and their fantastic writings.

Bess Rodriguez Richard

Ox of Vignales, Cuba acrylic on wood   30" x 40" 2009
collection of AAWR

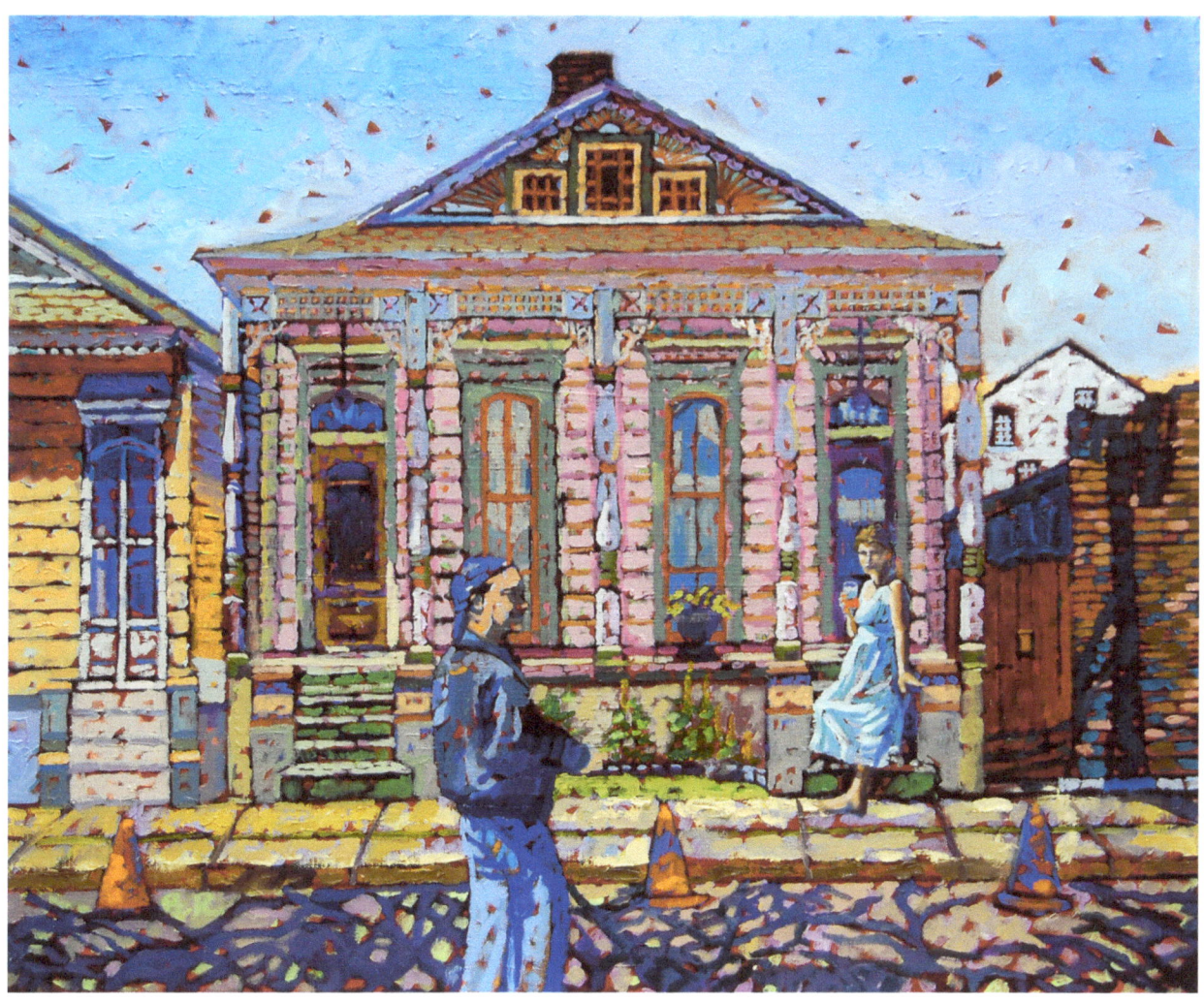

This painting follows a trend in my painting of looser and more broken brushwork. And a desire to create a setting and a story. So, I combined several photographs I'd taken of different sections of the Treme neighborhood (where jazz is said to have begun) in New Orleans, extracting parts I liked and incorporating and manipulating them. I added in an image of a woman to create a tension between her and the male figure.

Bess Rodriguez Richard

Treme, New Orleans, Louisiana acrylic and oil on canvas   20" x 24" 2013
collection of AAWR

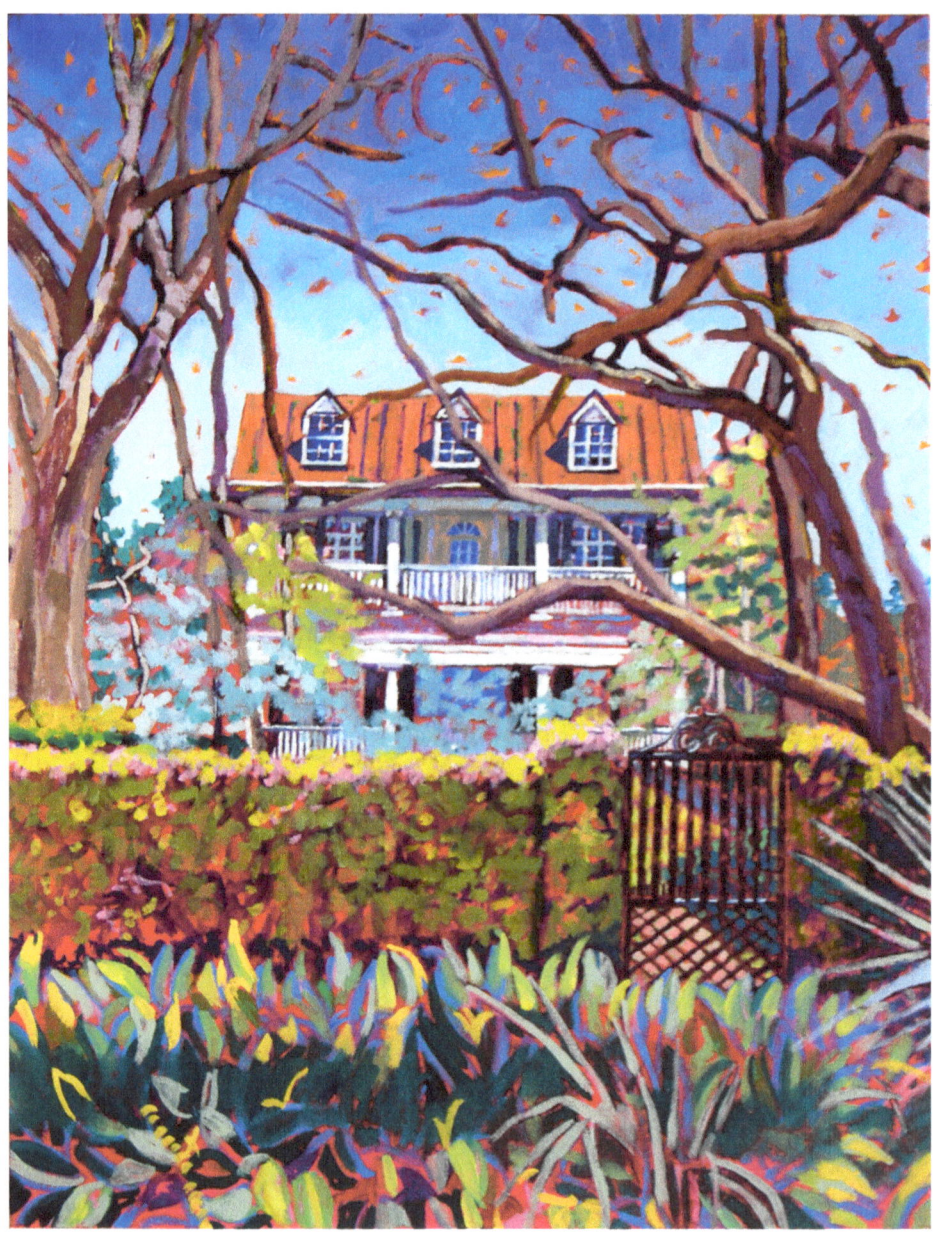

Last winter I visited Charleston, South Carolina. It had been more than 10 years since I first saw it. I love the old homes there and this one particularly. I exaggerated the tree branches in front and around the structure, creating a kind of web of mystery. And I left flecks of the red ground, something which I have done occasionally in other paintings, visible. These give the impression of leaves floating in the sky. And I chose to use a vertical format to make the scene more dramatic.

Bess Rodriguez Richard

Charleston Mansion, South Carolina acrylic and oil on canvas 24" x 18" 2018
collection of the artist

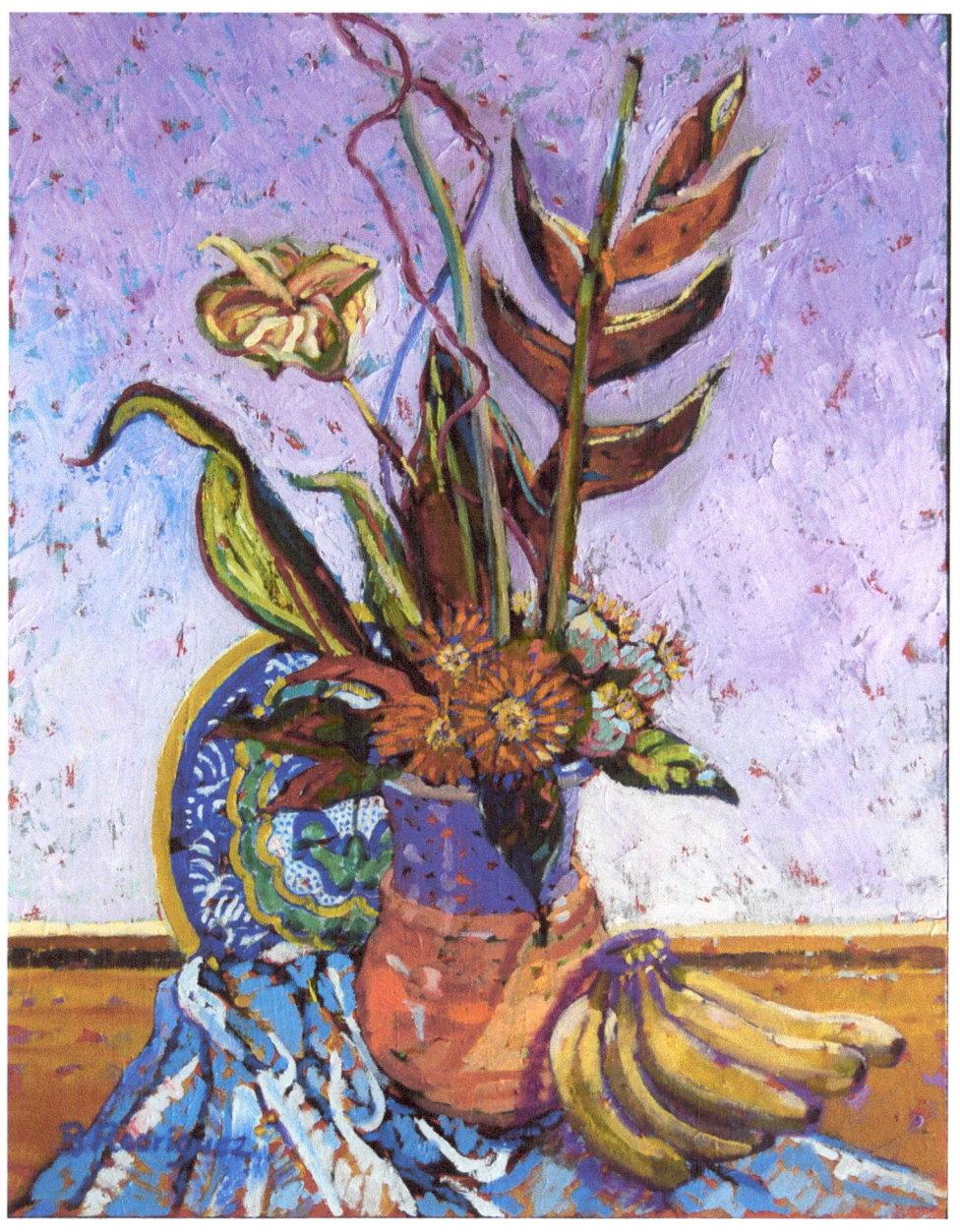

This painting is one of 4 with a floral subject but the only actual still life. And I tried to make it a tropical still life with vibrant flowers, bananas and a hand-painted ceramic plate with a red ground to accent and enliven. And I also built up the paint with a palette knife to give more texture.

Bess Rodriguez Richard

Tropical Still Life acrylic and oil and acrylic on canvas   24" x 30" 2013
collection of the artist

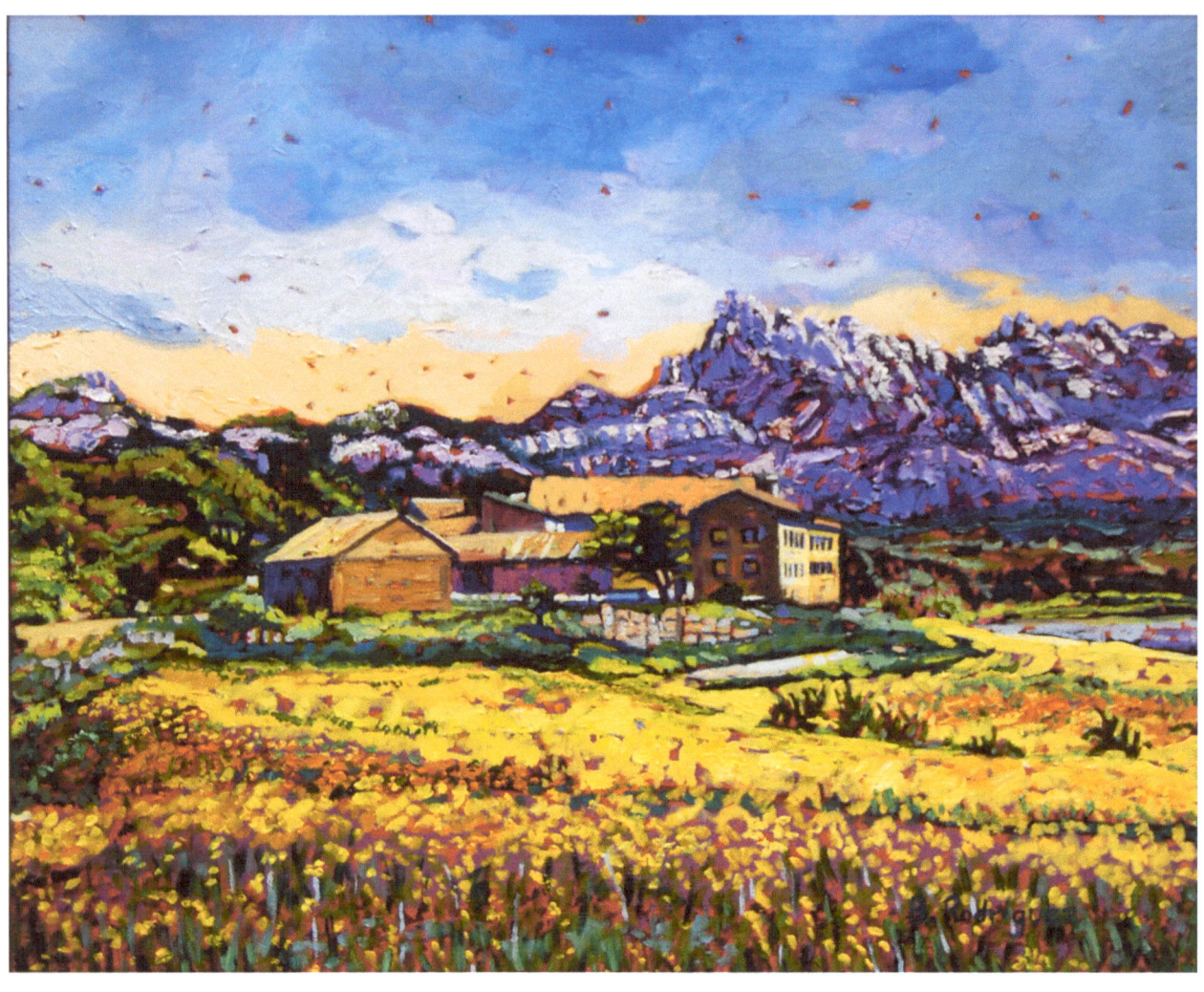

On a road trip from Bilbao to Barcelona, I saw a farm, or finca, as we were approaching Barcelona. There were stones in the fields that looked like roman ruins. And they probably were. I enjoyed building up vibrant layers of paint with brushes and palette knives and making the mountains as craggy as possible and the fields in the foreground dense with flowers.

Bess Rodriguez Richard

A Farm Outside Barcelona, Spain   acrylic and oil on canvas   20" x 24" 2014
collection of the artist

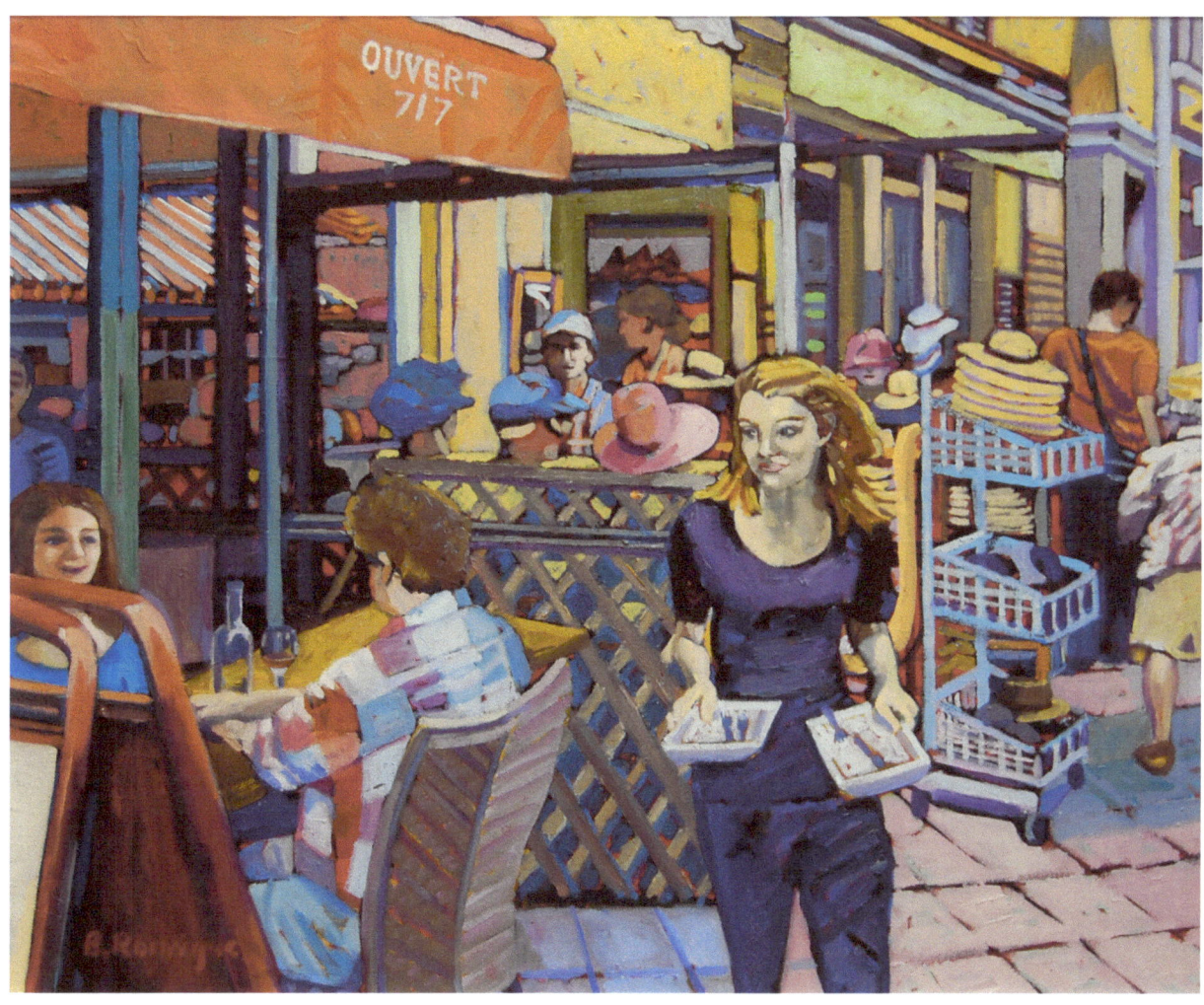

About 4 years ago, I visited Nice, France and went to a wonderful large market teeming with shops, restaurants and people. I snapped several photographs as memory aids when I returned to work in my studio. In this painting, I tried to capture the ocean breeze in the movement of the server's hair. To capture movement in 2-D was a challenge.

Bess Rodriguez Richard

Server in Motion, Nice, France   oil on canvas   20" x 24" 2017
collection of the artist

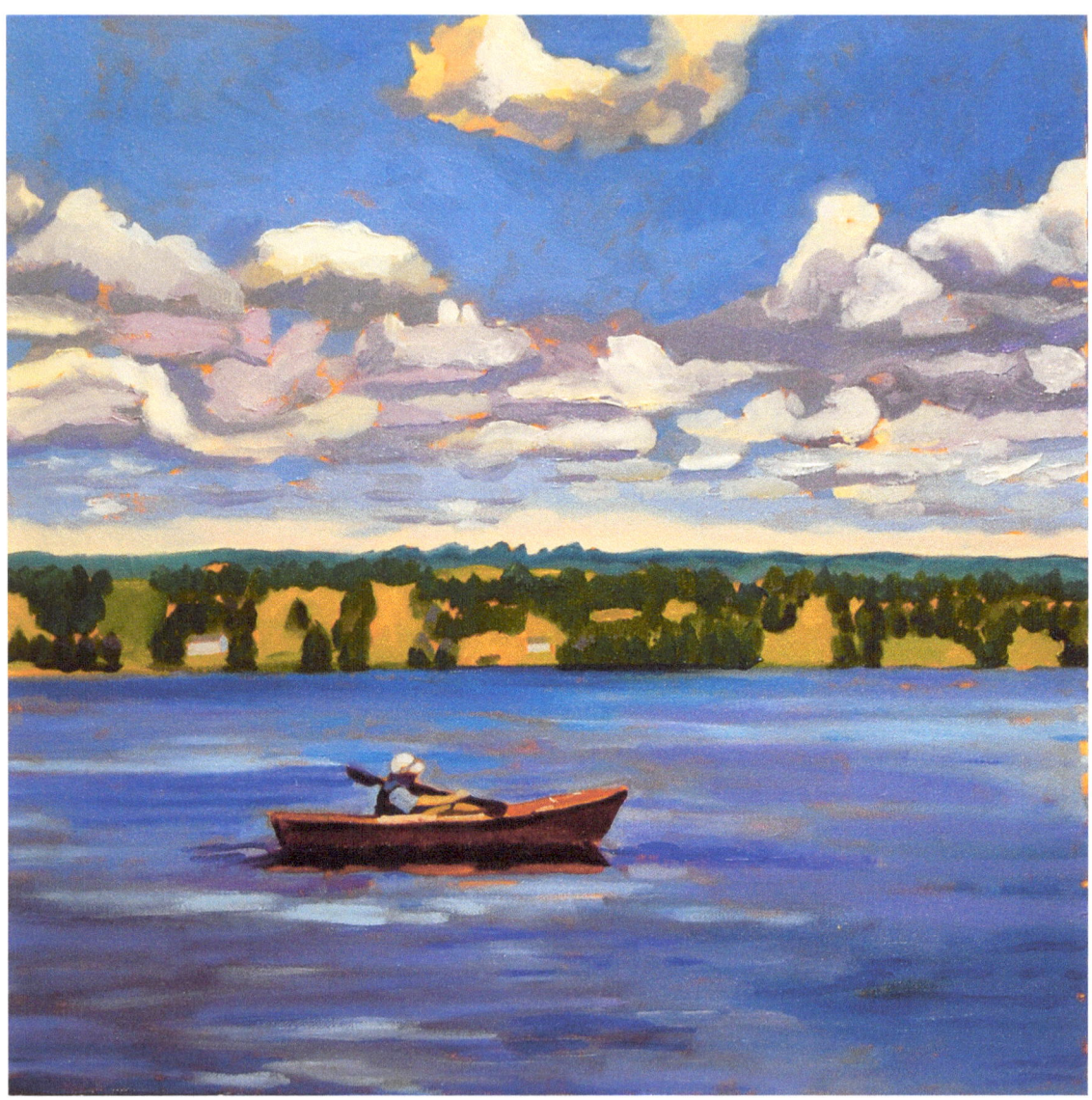

Both this painting and the sister painting, "Sailing on Lake Chautauqua", were painted at the same time. They are the same size and similar subject matter. I wanted to simplify the scene and create a kind of meditative experience for the viewer. So that one could place one's self in the kayak and feel the movement of the boat, the pull of the oar, and the sun beating down.

Bess Rodriguez Richard

Kayaking on Lake Chautauqua oil and acrylic on canvas   20" x 20" 2017
collection of the artist

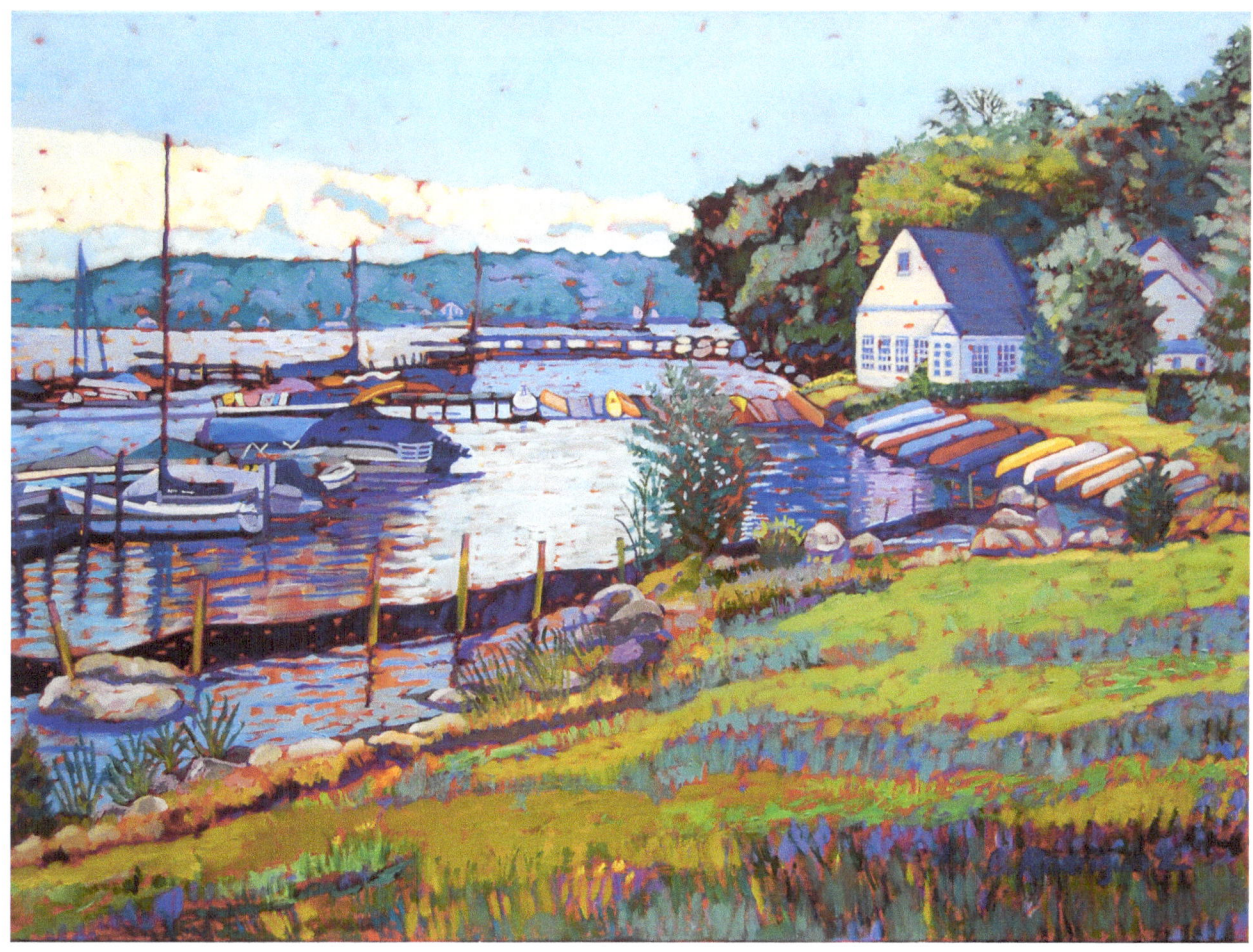

Years ago, an old friend introduced me to the Canadian Group of Seven painters' work at an exhibit in Ottawa's Art gallery. I loved their landscapes.... brilliant, vibrant, tactile, pleasing. And so, I tried to instill in this landscape a touch of them. Initially I'd left it much looser but reworked it at a later date and liked the final version.

Bess Rodriguez Richard

Chautauqua Marina   oil and acrylic on canvas   30" x 40" 2012 / 2014
collection of the artist

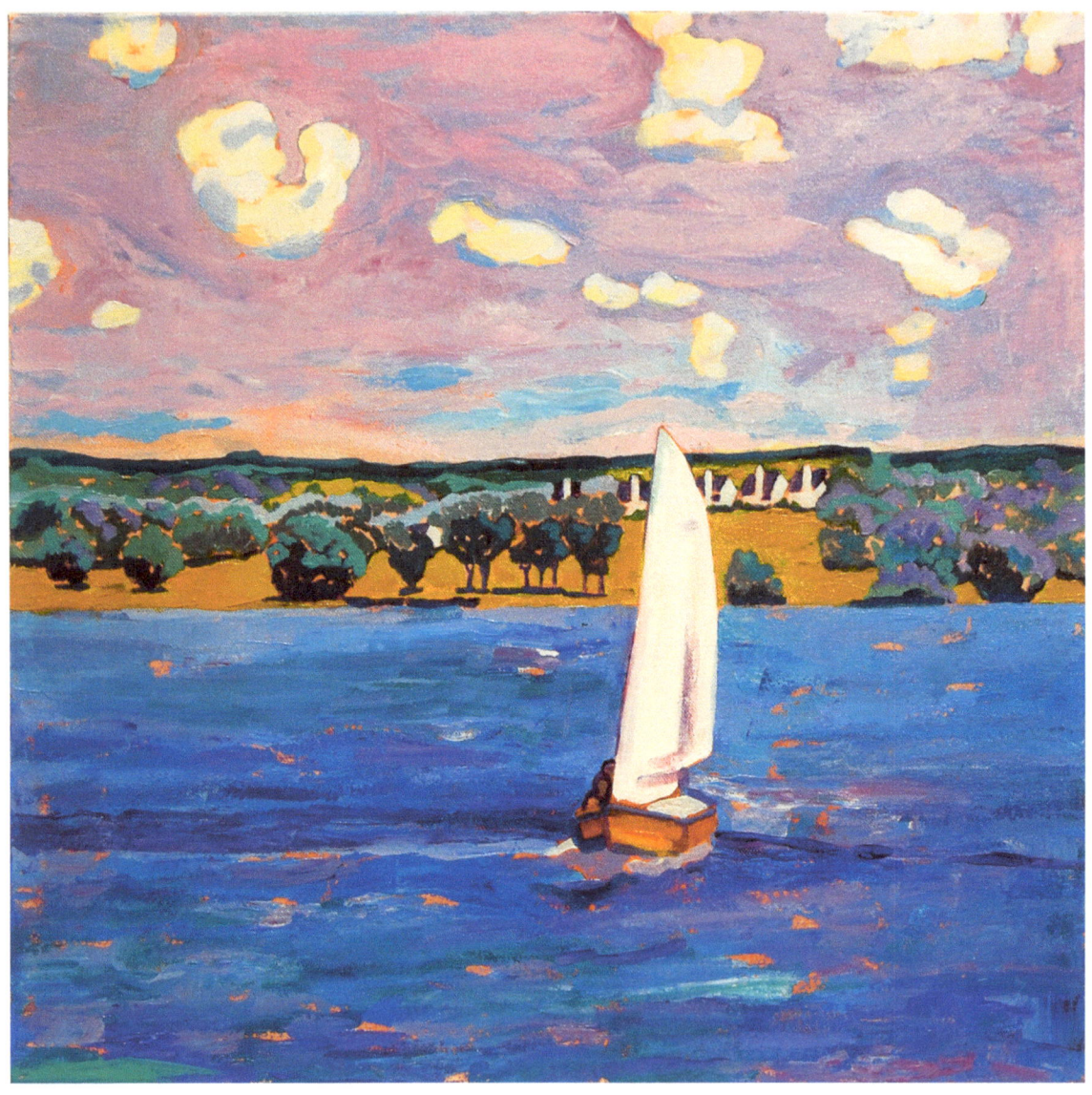

In this painting, I tried to be somewhat more abstract, by simplifying and reducing details and using a looser brushstroke with more impasto. At the same time, I tried to introduce a slightly whimsical tone in the sky color and cloud shapes. Of late, I spend some time in the summer at Chautauqua, New York and love to go boating on the lake there. The skies are so big, and the clouds are breathtaking.

Bess Rodriguez Richard

Sailing on Lake Chautauqua, New York   oil and acrylic on canvas   20" x 20" 2017
collection of the artist

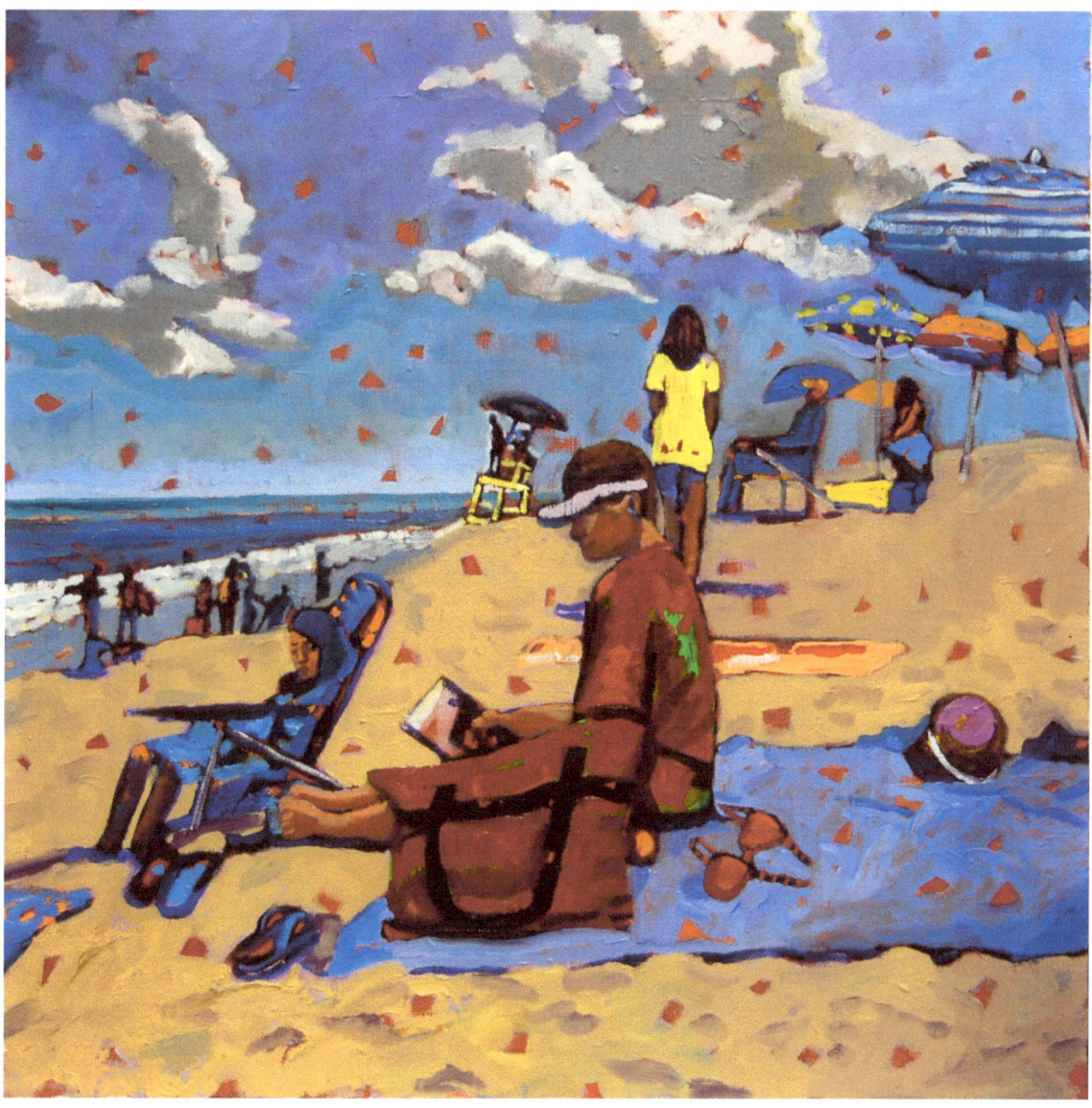

This is definitely one of my looser more expressive paintings. I spent many a summer at Bethany Beach and can still feel the wet sand under my feet.

Bess Rodriguez Richard

Bethany Beach, Delaware   acrylic on canvas   24" x 24" 2005
collection of the artist

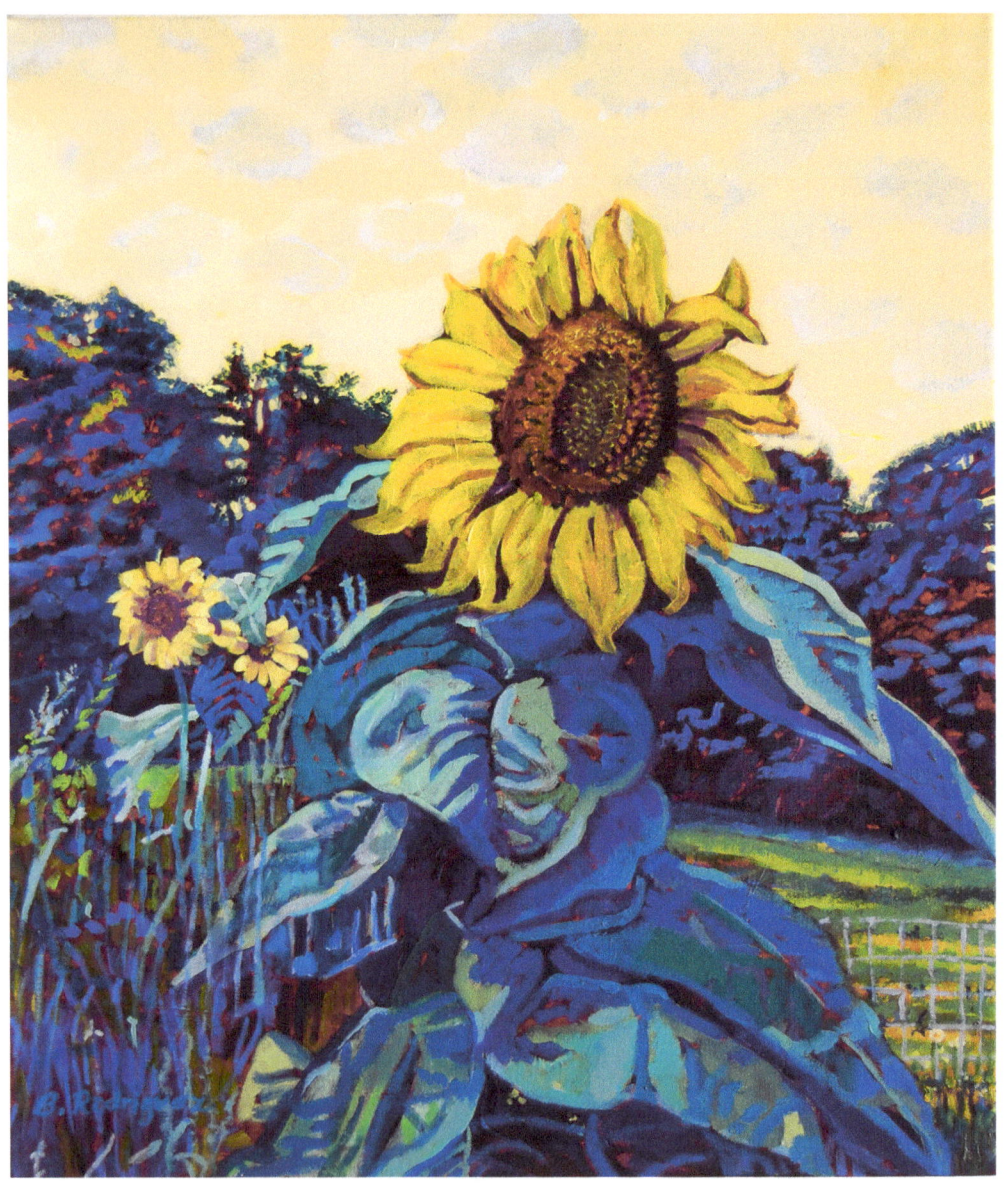

After my several eye surgeries, I visited a field of sunflowers in Chautauqua at a llama farm. And I took several photos, combined them, editing and deleting, until I came up with this fourth floral composition. One could say that the central sunflower represents a mother and the two smaller ones.... her children. And the large sunflower, Cyclopean, struggles to move onward.

Bess Rodriguez Richard

Sunflower, Marching oil and acrylic on canvas   24" x 20" 2015
collection of the artist

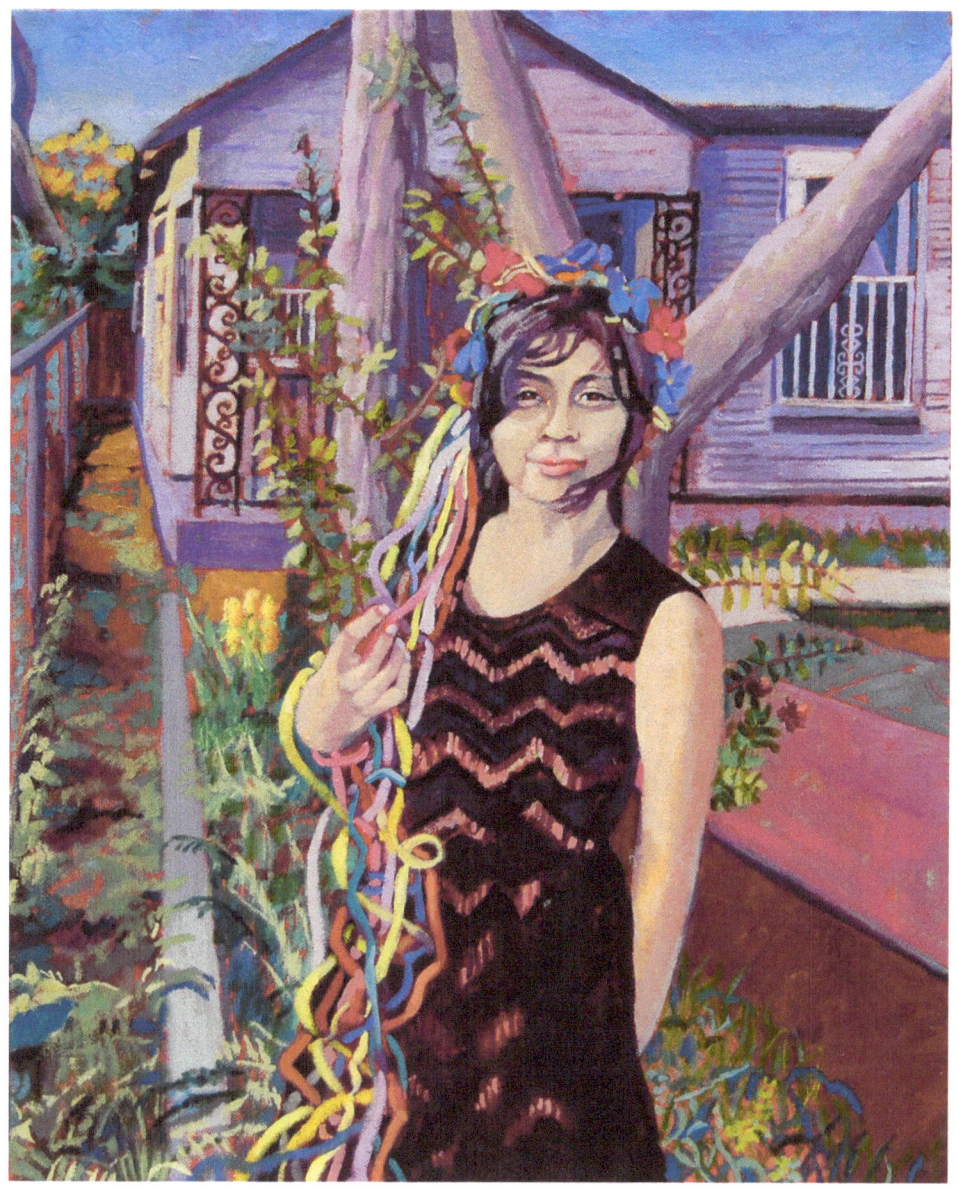

This little Mexican-American girl has had a rough life. One can invent an entire biography about her. But suffice it to say, she has had and will have a hard life. The expression on her face belies her youth but she's celebrating Fiesta Day wearing a headdress and streamers.

Bess Rodriguez Richard

Fiesta Girl, San Antonio, Texas oil and acrylic on canvas   20" x 16" 2018
collection of the artist

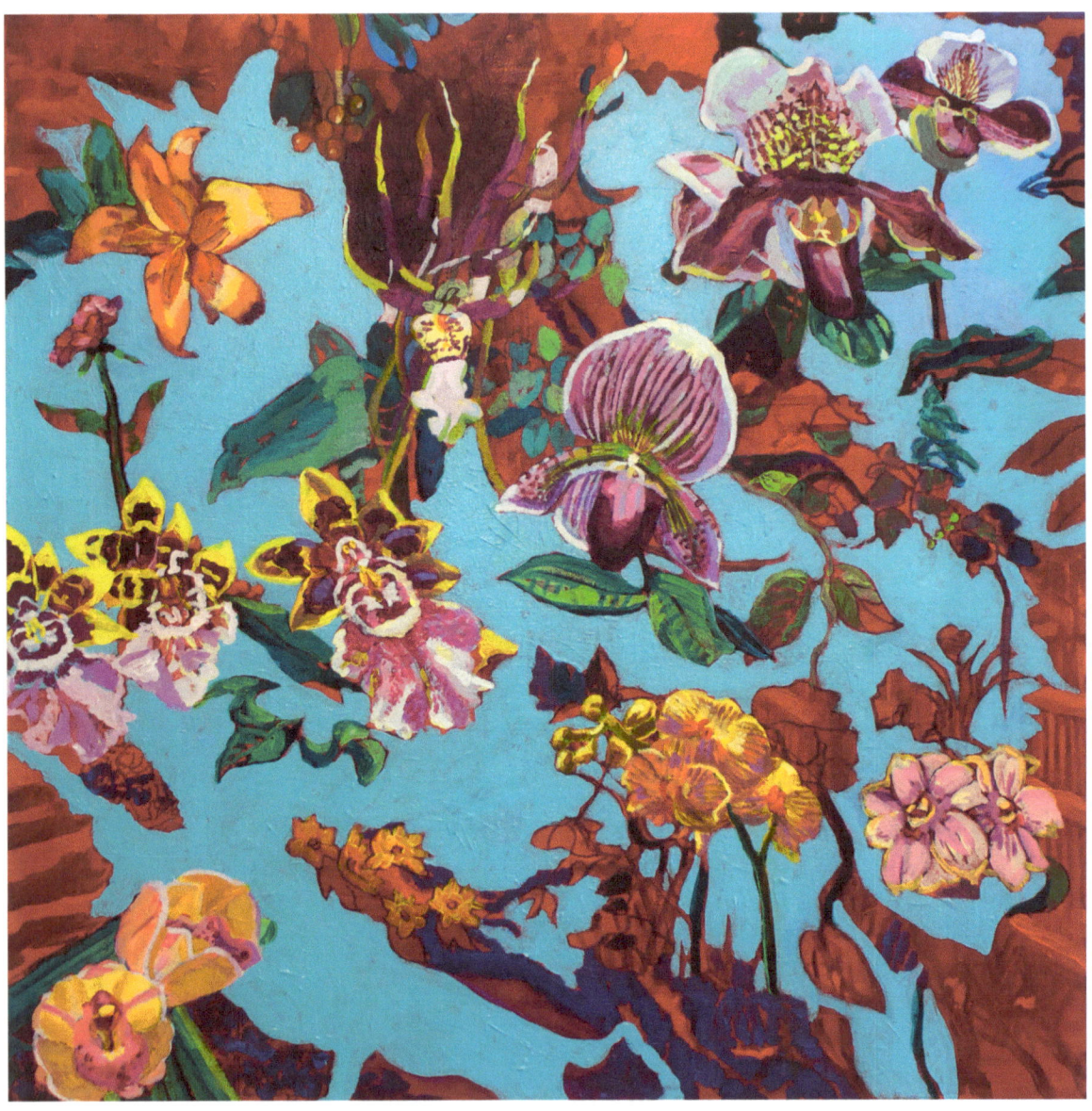

A few years ago, I underwent several eye surgeries and as I healed, found comfort and solace in painting flowers. I visited the Cleveland Botanical Garden "Orchid Mania" show and was inspired by the amazing variety of orchids and sensory experiences. I again created a somewhat abstract composition of the orchids. But, if you look closely you will see an "interloper" in the picture which I inserted to complete the composition. And I chose to use a particular blue to cut out the red ground and create a border.

Bess Rodriguez Richard

Orchid Blooms oil and acrylic on canvas   24" x 24" 2015
collection of the artist

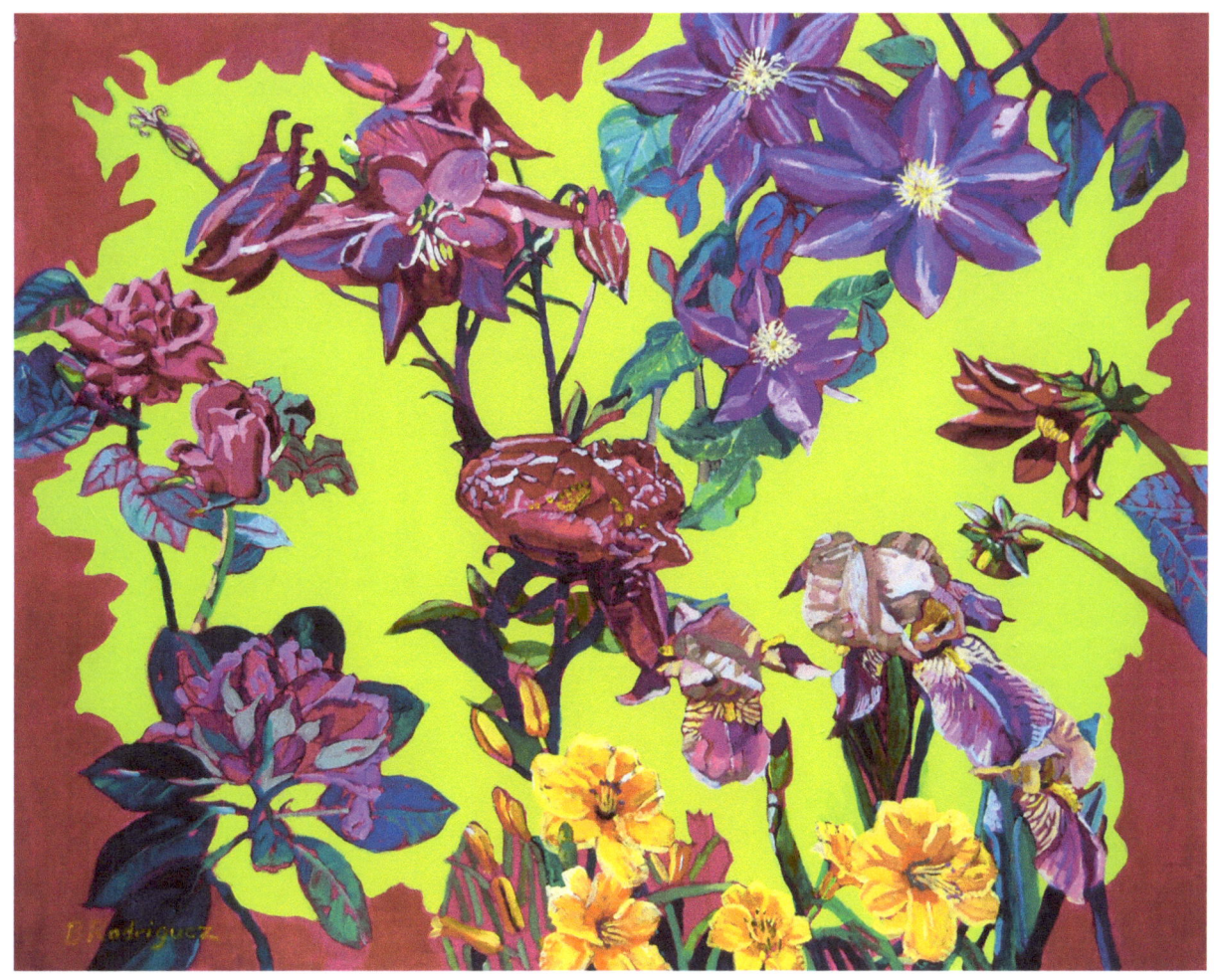

These flowers were from my garden. I like to describe it as a "Secret Garden", after Frances Hodgson Burnett's book of that name. Our garden is filled with many lovely flowers: clematis; dahlias; roses; lilies; irises; peonies and hibiscus...to name a few. We've tried to create a butterfly, hummingbird and honey bee haven, especially to keep the honey bees happy and prolific. I chose a different palette for this painting. Almost wanting to shock the viewer and cut out the magenta ground with a bilious green. I had seen algae growing on Horseshoe Lake nearby.

Bess Rodriguez Richard

Garden Blooms oil and acrylic on canvas   24" x 30" 2015
collection of the artist

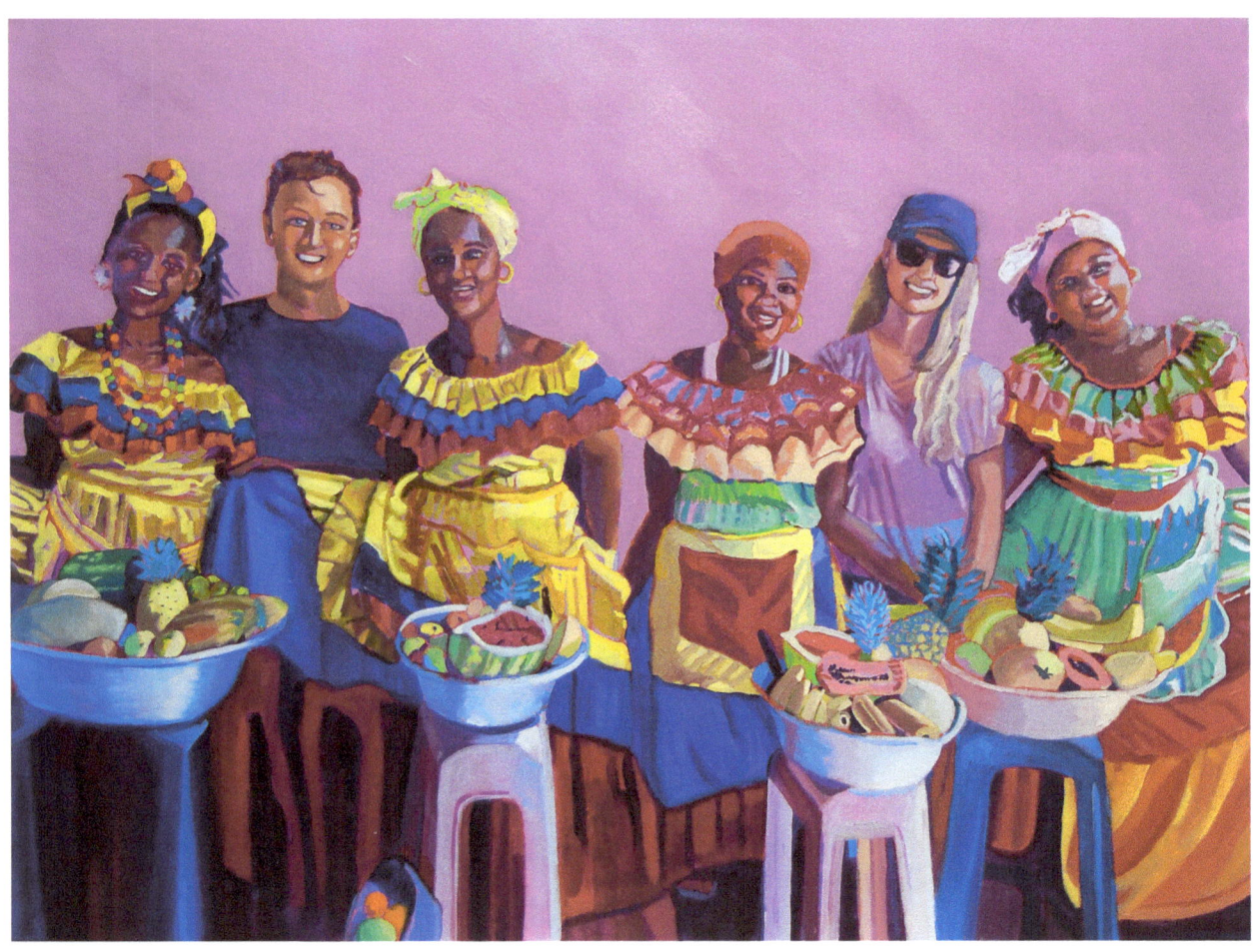

My son spent the summer in Bogota, Colombia and a fellow teacher joined him when he traveled to Cartagena. They were at a market one day and saw these "palenqueras", women of West African ancestry who speak a kind of creole. He asked if he could take photos with them. I liked the idea of these two peoples as a smiling, dancing group, and the concept of merging cultures. Before them, in bowls, are their produce for sale at a local market. I hope this painting makes the viewer as happy as it does the artist.

Bess Rodriguez Richard

Palenqueras and Gringos oil and acrylic on canvas   30" x 40" 2018
collection of the artist

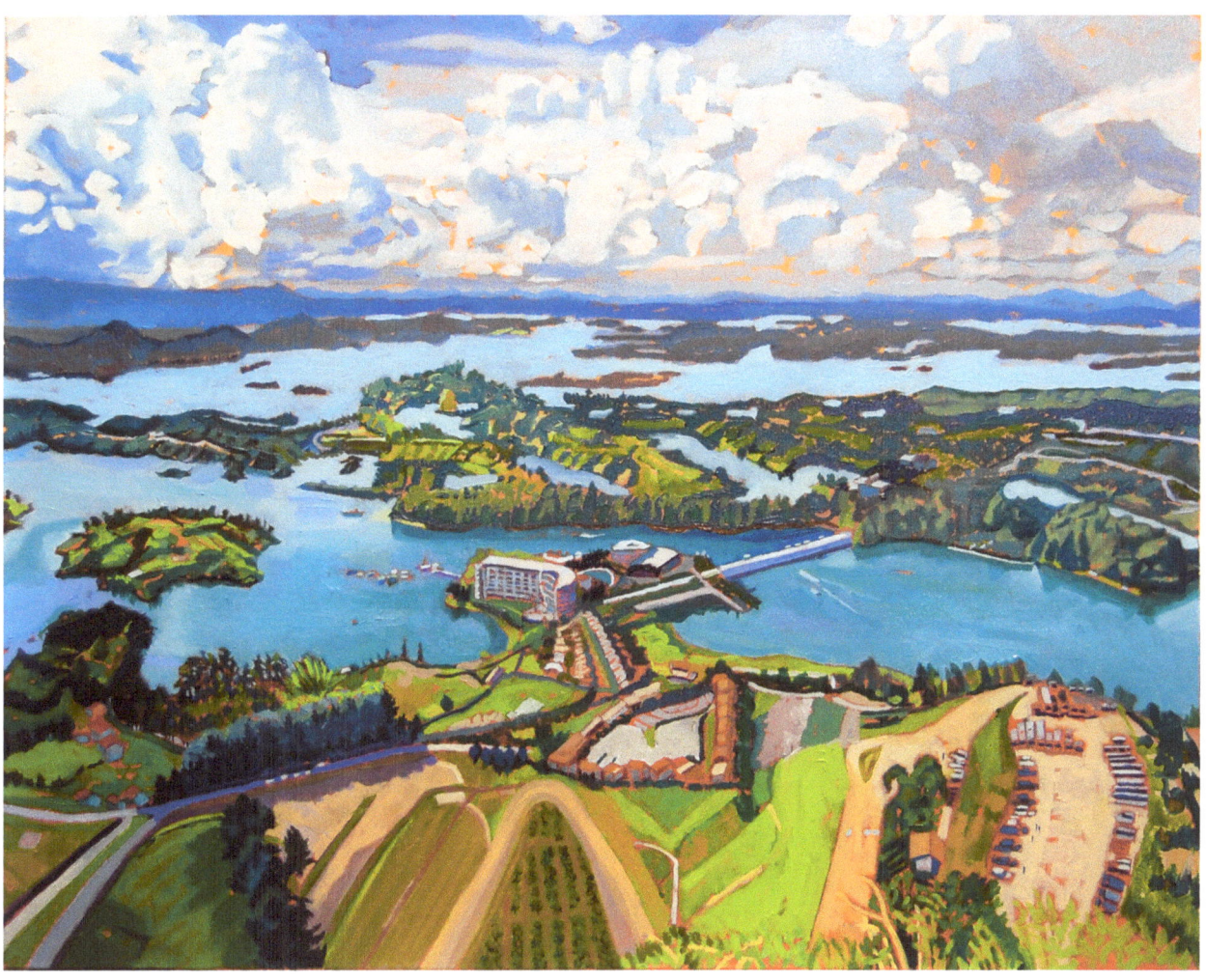

This painting depicts a bird's-eye view from the top of the Rock of Guatape, a landmark and tourist site in Colombia. I decided to use a two-tone ground: orange on the top half and red on the bottom half for this painting. And the sky I made into a kind of cloud study. It was for me a more abstract landscape of shapes than my norm of expressive landscapes.

Bess Rodriguez Richard

View from El Penon, Columbia oil and acrylic on canvas   24" x 30" 2018
collection of the artist

www.ingramcontent.com/pod-product-compliance
Lightning Source LLC
Chambersburg PA
CBHW051826210526
45473CB00005B/1756